Spray Your Swamp Cooler!

(and other words for the road)

Vol. 1

Albums by Tonemah

Ghosts of St. Augustine

A Time Like Now

One In Every Crowd

Welcome To Your Rainy Day

Ink Blots and Random Thoughts

Mulligan

A Moment in December

Spray Your Swamp Cooler!

(and other words for the road)

Vol. 1

Darryl P. Tonemah, Ph.D.

Brings Water Publishing

First Printing: 2014

ISBN 978-1-312-20873-5

Brings Water Publishing
PO Box 917
Lewiston NY 14092
www.Tonemah.com

Special discounts are available on quantity purchases by corporations, associations, educators, and others.

For details, contact Brings Water Publishing at the above listed address or
Tel: (405) 226-4434;
Fax: (716) 791 1312;
Email: BringsWaterPublishing@gmail.com

This book is dedicated to

My beautiful wifey and our three amazing kids
Thank you for who are you, all you do and your beautiful-ness.

My parents, Charles and Donna Tonemah, for their kindness
and guidance over a lifetime.

My brothers and sisters, David, Randy, Beth, Lisa, Gary, & LP
Thank you for your loving support.

To my friends over the years, who have offered
meals, couches, hugs and hope
All of you are represented in this book.

Tomee Brown, thank you for your patience and persistence. I
apologize for the contractions.

And most of all, Thanks and Glory to God; grace is *amazing*

Prologue

A little history

Have you ever heard of a swamp cooler? If you are under 40 years old and didn't visit my grandparents every summer when you were a child...in July...in Oklahoma, you may not have heard of one. Swamp coolers were what people used in the era between opening the window and air conditioning. It was the gateway air conditioner.

What you did with a swamp cooler was you sprayed the outside of it, (that part that stuck out of the window), with cold water, or however cool the water gets in a hose in Oklahoma in July. Ok, basically, you are spraying boiling water on the external parts of the swamp cooler. The *theory* was the act, of spraying it with water, cooled the air the fan was blowing inside the house, THUSLY, making the house cooler. In reality, it only made the person sitting on the opposite of the sprayer a little wet with second degree burns from the hot water. I believe it played out better in theory.

My experience with swamp coolers was that they didn't make things any cooler. They typically quadrupled the humidity within the house. So in Oklahoma, in July, if you quadrupled the humidity, you were basically living in a tropical rain forest, with the bonus of the occasional tornado!

Why do I have fond memories of swamp coolers? I'm glad you asked.

My grandparents grew up poor in rural Oklahoma. They were full blooded Native, Grandpa Kiowa, Grandma Comanche.

They were married, with six kidlets; my father being the second in line. They had tough times in those days. The kids worked, selling newspapers and picking cotton in Oklahoma heat, to bring in a little extra food money for the family.

At one point, Grandpa started his own business - Tonemah and Son Dirt Removal. He took out a loan for a bulldozer and he and my uncle worked hard to move dirt and dig ponds. They were never rich but they were paying their bills and were happy.

After years of moving dirt and paying their bills, my grandparents decided to move into town. There were paved roads and stop lights, the works!

Their house was small, two bedrooms and a tiny kitchen. It was theirs and they worked hard for it. They lived in town, with all of the hot pavement and the loud noise. Oklahoma summers are brutal, so Grandpa and Grandma decided to splurge on a creature comfort. They bought a used swamp cooler.

They unloaded it from their truck that was as old as Oklahoma, and struggled to put it in the front room window. They made sure it was close to the hose for practical purposes. Once installed, they stood in the living room and marveled at its pre-owned, gently loved, beauty.

They decided it was time for a test run. Grandpa went outside and fired up the hose. He waited about two hours for the water to cool down, and started soaking the swamp cooler. Grandma, ceremoniously, flipped the on switch inside the house. *SLIGHTLY* cooler, moist air sprayed dew on her face. Life was good.

As I write this, I remember my grandpa sitting on the couch in front of the swamp cooler, after a long day on the bulldozer, his shirt off, wearing just a t-shirt, basking in the glow of the cooler moist air. That swamp cooler meant so much more to him than a minor convenience purchased with his hard work. He was taking care of what was taking care of him - the swamp cooler, his work, their home, and my grandma.

I realized the significance of this as an adult. I now have a wifey, a few kidlets, and a couple of car payments. I need to look after what needs looking after. My grandpa never came out and told me this stuff. By observing him and my grandma, later observing my father and my mother, and now my wife and kids, I see there are so many lessons going on in a million places a million ways every day. We just need to open up to them.

My grandparents, overtly and subtly, passed their knowledge to my father, who did the same for me. His more common wise-isms include "You can't soar with the eagles if you are up hootin' with the owls" and "Son, you have to have enough sense to pour pee out of a boot." The latter was more of a metaphor, (I hope), but pouring out whatever is in your boot before you put it on is pretty solid advice. I think he was saying, "Try to do things that make sense for you, Darryl." Don't be dumb.

My mother, on the other hand, was more of a practical advice giver, no need to dabble in the esoteric. Anything that was in the newspaper or on the news became part of her daily goodbye. "Have a good day, son, I love you...watch out for other drivers, they are crrrazy...don't get hit by lightning…don't run over a buffalo…don't get bitten by a disease-carrying fly." You get the picture. Goodbyes took a while. She gives practical advice. I love it.

I didn't ramp up into the "advice giving process", especially the advice that means the most, the kind that carries itself into the next generation. The moment when my first child was dropped into my lap, I realized my heart had a whole new gear I wasn't aware of. All of the lessons, subtly and overtly taught to me, by so many amazing people over the years, suddenly counted. Thankfully, I had, and still have, great role models.

When I had kidlets, there was desperation to love them and care for them and teach them and everything else my mom warned me about. I didn't have kids as a young guy. I wasn't old either, I was a *tweener*. But as I write this, I have friends younger than me who are grandparents and others who have kids well into college. I have a 2 year old son. He doesn't have kids of his own, and he isn't in college. I also have a 6 year old son and a 10 year old daughter, who are also kidless and degreeless. But I can unbiasedly say they are the best kids on earth. Yup, number 1.

I'm writing this book to them, for them. The words in this book were inspired by them.

It is rooted in the first day my daughter, Gracie, was to start pre-k. It started the night before. It was five autumns ago.

As the frost was on the pumpkin and the hay was in the barn (thanks, James Taylor), I became excited for her to explore new worlds. I wanted to talk with her after school and ask her how was her day, and what did you learn. I imagined my 4 year old would offer me witty anecdotes about how Elmo was right all along, and Kermit and Miss Piggy just wouldn't work out for a plethora of reasons. These were wonderful dreams, until it came time for her to wake up on the first day of school.

I ran into the bedroom of my little princess and expected her to be wide awake and anxious to begin her academic career! I nuzzled up to her and said "Time to wake up, sunshine". My little Ms. Brightside didn't budge. The kind of "didn't budge" that I could tell she purposely wasn't budging. It was intentional *budgelessness*. It seemed to be her belief that if she played possum, both school and I would go away.

Rather than jolt her into the new routine, I fired a couple of warning shots, "Time to start thinking about waking up baby girl, you don't have to act on it yet, but put it in the hopper." After my third try, I realized I would have to take the initiative in getting this ball rolling, knowing she would come around once she was out of bed. So, I picked her up, thinking that she would snap to attention and start her day. Unfortunately, she went with the noodle spine defense. It was like I picked up a precious, beautiful, wet towel. It is amazing how much weight a person can put on when they go noodle spine!

My dad logic was, I'll prime the pump and she'll get rolling in a second. So I propped her over the sink and gently washed her face and peeled her lips back and moved her head while I brushed her teeth. She STILL pretended to be asleep. I had to admire her conviction! Not until we got into the car to head to school did she decide to open her eyes, and fill them with tears, big, huge, humongous gushers, big fellers! She didn't bellow; it was just the silent breaking heart, that kind that crushes the defenses of a daddy. Sara Groves has a song, "He looks like Charles Bronson when he cries…" I'd say that applies here, to me, not her.

I had thought about just turning left and heading to a state where they have more lenient truancy laws. But realized I really hadn't done my research on that topic. So I spent the 20 minute drive trying to distract her (me) from her (my) breaking heart. I pointed out ridiculous things like "Look hon, a water tower!!" saying it with ridiculously inappropriate conviction. "Honey, a car dealership!!!" These futile attempts didn't even come close to working; out of desperation, I said "let's see who can make the funniest face." It stopped the crying (from both of us), but set an awful precedent. It's a game we still play to this day.

Having achieved the goal of getting her to stop crying, I felt comfortable keeping her within the local school system. We sat outside of her school for a few minutes, working up the courage to go inside (me, not her). She started a soft, heartbreaking sniffle again. I opened her door and unbuckled her from her car seat. I was getting ready to share my baby girl with the world. She draped onto me and put her head on my shoulder, soaking it with her impressively large tears. At some point you'd think she'd get dehydrated. I was worried she would cramp up.

I walked her to her class. There were several other kids struggling with abandonment issues. Their parents and I looked at each other and gave an "I know what you're going through" face. At least I think that's the face I made. My cheeks were still pretty numb from face making in the car.

I wanted to say something to her, to let her know she is never ever alone. I kneeled next to her and hugged her. I held her hand, and said,

"Baby Girl?"

"Yes, Daddy?"

"I love you with all my heart every second of my life."

"I love you too, Daddy."

"Some things are scary, aren't they?"

"I don't want to go to school."

"School will help your brain get all wrinkly."

Puzzled look.

I said, "Honey, when you are feeling scared, get prayed up, have a strong heart, focus, and try try try."

What does that mean!? I asked myself.

At that moment, I didn't know what it meant. I just knew I wanted her to lean on God. I wanted her to believe in the strength she gets from that relationship. I wanted her to feel powerful and safe. I wanted her to be more powerful than her fear. I wanted her to protect her soul. I wanted her to find her passion. I wanted her to be the best version of herself no matter what is going on around her. I wanted her to pursue things that are important to her with the same conviction she used to execute noodle spine. I wanted her to grow up happy, and feel loved, and supported. But how do I say that to a 4 year old ten seconds before I release her to the world? On a daily basis, as a parent, it is my job to demonstrate and model that for her. But preschool is just the beginning of her leaving the house. So I repeated it.

"Get prayed up."

"Have a strong heart."

"Focus."

"Try Try Try."

I made her say it after me.

"Baby girl, if you are feel a little scared today remember, say it again."

"Get prayed up."

"Have a strong heart."

"Focus."

"Try Try Try."

She turned and looked back at me while she was walking into her class. I'm not sure who had a bigger lump in their throat, her or me. This is just the beginning of so many goodbyes.

Get prayed up.

Have a strong heart.

Focus.

Try Try Try.

Protect your soul, baby girl.

I left her at preschool that day, to the savage world of sack lunches and nap times.

I sat in the car and tried to recompose myself. Journey's song, "Separate Ways," was on the radio. You're killin' me Steve Perry, with your touching lyrics and soulful voice!

I drove out of the parking lot on my way to work, on my way to a job that I didn't particularly like but wanted to do well.

Get prayed up.

Have a strong heart.

Focus.

Try Try Try.

I realize the phrase came so easily to me because I wasn't necessarily talking to her. It was something that I needed to hear and believe in for myself. Whenever I tried something new, or different, or uncomfortable, I needed to hear it. Whenever I stepped into a new opportunity, I needed to hear it. When I was experiencing life's little tornados, I needed to hear it. It helped me through the day, and it helped her through the day.

I hugged her when I saw her when I got home that evening.

I asked her,

"How'd school go?"

"It was FUN! Did you know Alex's dog is named Scooby?!"

In my mind- Nope, who is Alex? That sounds like a boy's name. Never talk to him. Never talk to any boy. Ever. As long as you live.

What came out of my mouth was, "No, how cool!"

Ahhh…Youth. From tragedy to triumph. Thanks Scooby.

She made it through her school day. I made it through my work day.

Honestly, life is good. God is good.

Our little phrase has become our little goodbye ritual since that first day of school. Her little brother, Parks, is now part of the fold, and in a few years their baby brother, Jack Jack, will go to school. They know why I say it and why we believe it.

I've written our little saying on graduation cards for my nieces and nephews as they are heading off to college. I've also written it to friends starting new adventures in their lives. It has more or less become a philosophy of life in our home. I have had the chance over the last few years to think about it a little more and flesh it out. It has been part of graduation addresses I've given and groups I've spoken to. This little book is what I have come up with.

There are a bazillion motivational or self-help books out there. This isn't one of them. I am going to assume you are already motivated. The question is for what are you motivated? Feeling empowered helps with your decisional balance. I just want to cheer you on.

Everything that follows is a little lesson from so many amazing people in my life. My influences include my ancestors who sacrificed and lived and died to have a voice and opportunity; my grandparents; my parents, my siblings, my wifey and my kidlets, and my friends. All these people have voices in this book.

Oh, Yeah, if you don't believe in the power of prayer, read for a while and see how it goes.

Darryl

Thing One - On Purpose

Get Prayed Up

I hope you have good lives. I hope things go your way often, but not all the time. Sometimes you need the tough times to see what you have under the hood. Hopefully you look under the hood and see it was God making the engine go all along.

Pray before your feet hit the floor in the morning. Be thankful. For everything, life, breath, challenges, family, food, etc. I've got an idea. You don't have to be thankful for the things that God doesn't provide (ha! Think about it!). Pray for guidance, pray for protection, pray for loved ones. I saw something on Facebook, (don't go there for knowledge please), and it said "What if the things that you didn't pray for today, weren't here tomorrow".

Be prayerful. It doesn't have to be perfect or beautiful. God will just be happy to hear from you.

God has had this moment, this day, planned long before your beautiful face felt the sunshine. He has the whole deal planned. You just need to jump on board. Once you understand that the whole thing is worked out, you just need to be a part of it, put your "yes" on the table. You can be used in some amazing ways! Maybe it's something you do or say, or a way you act or your attitude that is a blessing to someone that somehow changes something. Sadly in any given moment, it ain't all about you. If you believe that something good can happen, just wait and go with it.

Remarkable things can

happen when your

"yes"

is on the table.

There are healthy risks and

there are unhealthy risks.

Know the difference.

You have no idea what challenges or opportunities are coming today. It is a scary proposition to get out of bed without being prayed up. If you wait until the lil' tornados of life happen and hope to get through them, you are being reactive rather than proactive. Build your life on a solid foundation. So what could have been lil' tornados are now just gentle breezes. Go fly a kite in them!

God opens doors when he knows you are ready for them. You may not believe you are ready. That's why we pray.

God knows much more about you than you do and sees things to the end. We can only see what is immediately in front of us, which is a blessing. I wouldn't be smart enough to handle knowing the future! I'd always be asking "DUDE, WHERE ARE THE FLYING CARS?!?!"

Going with that plan is called faith. Have faith. Sometimes the answer is yes, sometimes it's no, sometimes it's wait, I've got you covered. If the answer is No or WAIT, keep breathing. There is a plan. You are praying to God, not Santa Claus.

If we truly believe that life, that eternity, is made up of a bazillion little moments, then one little moment doesn't define you. Don't define yourself by your weakest moments. You are the habits and arc of character over your lifetime.

When lil' tornados occur in your life,

or in your day,

breathe for a moment.

Don't react.

Pray.

Be calm in your heart.

Believe that things happen in God's time and part of God's plan. It may not be obvious to us, and it may make no sense to us at the time. That's probably why we aren't in charge. The other day I was watching a documentary about the group, The Eagles. They were a pretty chaotic band, but their music was good and things worked out in the end. Their guitarist, Joe Walsh, said "In the middle of it, it all looked like chaos but looking back at it over the years, it looked like a beautifully crafted novel." God knows how it ends. That is called faith. Have faith.

Be powerful. So many outlets are trying to brainwash us today, trying to have us believe that the word *power* refers to what you wear, what you drive, and what you have. And every single one of those things can be washed away in 6 inches of water, buried in a foot of snow, or blown away by a strong breeze.

Those who believe the

irrational definition

of power are defining

themselves by their

weakest attributes.

Stuff.

Understand that power is not those things at all. It never has been and never will be. Many have created and praise their lesser gods. Power is a character trait and we are sometimes blessed to be the conduit God uses to lift those around us, to be the hands and feet and voice of caring. The person who understands this as powerful, doesn't seek power but is attributed that characteristic, when we give and love. You were created to serve, to be of value.

Get prayed up.

Be powerful.

We make mistakes, sometimes big ones.

Seek forgiveness.

Forgive yourself.

Next Thing

Have a Strong Heart

I propose this: You were made for a purpose on purpose, designed purposefully. You have all the tools you need to do what God put you here to do. That includes your looks, your height, your hair, you skin, your family, the whole deal. That is pretty amazing. You look how you're supposed to look! Some other tools are in seed form, you need to help them develop, prayerfully. Maybe through education (in all forms) and effort, sometimes tears. Max out the gifts God gave you. If they were just handed to you, in full awesome form, you may not appreciate them as much.

I have known many naturally gifted students, athletes, musicians who didn't appreciate and nurture their God given gifts. They chose to be average by not committing to nurture their gifts. They could have been great.

Unrealized potential is a sad thing.

On the flip side of that, I have seen people who aren't so naturally gifted, but put the time, effort, and sweat in, to became great. It's those people who excite me! They don't have an ounce of entitlement. These people believe that what they have prayed on, and set their heart to, is only time and effort away.

God gives this determination. It's a gift.

If everything came easy,

we would appreciate very little.

Now this may just be me talking, but if the above scenario is true, you are prayed up, your heart is in the right place, and God has challenged you to achieve. It's time to put on your big boy/girl pants and get after it.

Honestly, there will be a million reasons to not pursue a goal. Too hard, too long, too much time, too hot, too cold, too just right! You need to stick to the one or two reasons to achieve. That is your true north. Follow that and it'll get you there. Keep praying along the way, because what we perceive as the true end, may be what we need to see so we keep moving forward. Keep open to the thought that God's purpose in it was for us to influence, effect, change a life somewhere along the way. That may be the TRUE end...for God's purpose.

That's why we pray.

We've all seen or heard the folks saying (or we've watched Flashdance), it is my true calling to be the biggest most famous star on earth, to be in movies, to be the biggest rock star. I know that is why I am here......(long nasal sigh). I'm not sure that is true. So many people say that if it occurred for everyone, there would be nobody left to actually attend the movies or go to the concerts. Are they truly prayed up on it and listening for a true answer? Or are they/we listening for the answer we hope to hear so we manufacture it? There is probably a difference.

I play music. When I first started, I wanted to be the Native Bruce Springsteen. I could picture it. I strummed my lil' guitar...I wrote lil' love songs...I wore a bandana in my back pocket...put gel in my hair and then messed it up the appropriate amount. These were all the prerequisites to making myself a STAR.

I'm glad it didn't happen.

The biggest blessing in my life was that
the answer to that prayer was no.

As hard as I pushed my own agenda, God made sure the right agenda occurred. I have a great life, a beautiful wife, and great kids. Things aren't always easy but that's part of the deal. Just like the wise philosopher, Joe Walsh, said, "…in retrospect it looks like a finely crafted novel."

Although, if it did happen, I would've ROCKED YOUR WORLD! Just sayin'...

It's when we start doubting our tools, and looking at what other people have in their toolbox, is when we start feeling weaker, or jealous, envious. Don't do that.

Don't ever feel less than anyone else.

Maximize the tools you have.

You decide who your audience is. If you worry about everyone's opinion, you're going to FREAK yourself out with stress. Surround yourself with people who love you and are honest with you.

The most important audience

is an audience of one.

Money, athletic ability, better academics, etc., are all just stuff. At some point you will have more or less, or better or worse. Approach it all prayerfully and with humility. You be the best version of you.

Be your "Ness."

What the heck does that mean?!?!

I'm glad you asked.

We are all born with a certain character trait the makes us totally unique. Maybe it's a collection of character traits. That is your "Ness". Your (Put your name here)-*NESS*. For the longest time I thought my *Ness* was WEIRD-Ness. Then I realize this is how I am wired. I have actually come to embrace it.

ROCK YOUR "NESS"!!

Protect your soul. There is so much in the world that wants to pick away at you. Sometimes it can be a sad, hurtful, angry place. You decide who you are going to be, don't give that power to someone else. You are amazing and loved and appreciated. Don't let lesser things chip away at that. Know deep in your soul that you are never alone.

Still, small moments are

valuable and beautiful.

You will never overuse the words
"Please" and "Thank you."

Keep a historical perspective. There have been so many people before you that prayed up and stayed strong. Those people gave you the opportunity to sit and read this book. It's not accidental. Your grandparents, their grandparents, and their grandparents and so on and so on, survived and thrived so you can have opportunities. You think you have tough times? They had no internet! Look at your history books (ha!), I mean, google how your ancestors lived. That will truly give us perspective and appreciate the fact that they paved the roads (literally and metaphorically) that we so easily travel today.

Have a strong heart and gentle hands.

Apologize.

Get prayed up and have a strong heart.

Another Part

Focus

This little part is more practical than theoretical. The next TWO parts are practical applications once you get rolling. I guess that makes sense because you have to build on a solid foundation. So our foundation has been praying and strength. That's a pretty good way to start anything! Try to make Mac and Cheese without prayer and strength....or without cheese and noodles.

It's very difficult!

I thought about writing a cool metaphor about lasers, and focus, or how focused fog can fill one cup of water. But that's not where I want to go. I want to encourage you to set some specific goals, after getting prayed up. Set your sights. If you believe truly that it is a goal you are to be headed toward. Make change into small doable doses.

Break the process into

small things over time.

Why are you choosing this goal? Write it down.

When you are frustrated or angry or hurt, go back and

look at what you wrote. It will be a short quick

reminder.

Keep praying.

While working toward your goal, behave well. People that you don't even know are watching you. You are representing yourself and your family and many other people.

Do good things, do hard things, say good things, believe good things.

Keep yourself balanced.

Your goal is a part of your life,

it isn't your life.

Know your benchmarks. How do you know you are moving forward? Set specific benchmarks when leaning toward your goal. Know when you are moving toward your final goal. Remember each inch forward is a success because you aren't moving backward.

Sometimes your pace isn't God's pace.

Continue to pay attention to what you do well and good. Continue to grow those things. Those may be the tools God wants to use in you. If there is something you don't do particularly well, don't beat yourself up. You are set up for exactly the gifts you need to bring this thing in!

What are you most motivated for? Check your bank account. That will tell you where you spend your money. Look at how you spend your time in the day. That will tell you what your priorities are. We spend time doing what is most important to us at any given moment. Generally hanging on Facebook isn't going to get you where you need to be, (unless your goal is to be on Facebook, then CONGRATULATIONS! YOU'RE THERE!). Prioritize the important stuff in your day, and then do the other stuff when you have a moment.

We are motivated for

whatever we are doing;

otherwise we would do something else.

Focus.

Do what you gotta do

for as long as you gotta do it.

Then play!

When you're done,

recreate,

laugh,

run,

love,

play,

stomp in mud puddles.

Be sure to put play in your day

whatever your age!

Choose your mood!

You may not have control of everything around you. But you have control of your attitude. Think good things! Think positive things! Think powerful thoughts! Pray!

Last thing

Try Try Try

I think it was Yoda who said, "Try not. Do or do not. There is no try." First of all, maybe he's wrong, who knows, he's not from around here. When I say "Try Try Try", I am talking about the exertion of effort. Continue to exert effort toward your goal. Exert effort, exert effort, exert effort doesn't sound as cool as try, try, try.

If you have done your *praying up* and are convinced, not of your own devices, but that it is God's will that you do this, try. If that doesn't work, try again. And if that doesn't work, try again. Keep trying. Quite possibly, we reach the goal. Maybe we aren't to achieve this particular goal but we gain something greater. We learned how to be persistent, to *TRY*. We learn what it feels like to struggle and try, and to keep swinging away. Maybe sometimes that is the lesson. If you learn that lesson, possibly the goal you had to learn it for, will be coming soon.

Know where your need ends

and God's will begins.

Things may be working at a 90 degree angle. You may be presented with a challenge and you are up to the task. You get after it, and get after it, and get after it. Yet it seems like you are "Dancing in the Dark" (Thanks, Bruce!). Sadly, maybe it's not all about you. Someone sees your heart and your effort, and they tell someone, who tells someone, who knows someone who needs to be cheered on. You have NO IDEA who that person is or that they exist, but you have been a positive influence on them. That's awesome.

Do Good Things.

You are blessed to be a blessing. It may not be financially or athletically, or possibly in other ways. Maybe you are blessed at any given moment, with a good attitude that can be a blessing for someone else.

Be grateful that you even have the opportunity to try. Did you know that there are people right here in your town, that would love the opportunity to try, to swing away, but for whatever reason, for whatever circumstance, they aren't? You are gifted with the opportunity. Swing away.

Be grateful.

The more you are grateful, the more you realize there is more to be grateful for.

Smile

Lots

See what happens.

Spray your swamp cooler.

Epilogue

This book doesn't have all the answers. Maybe it doesn't have the answers that you are looking for. But between this book, the people who love you, the people who support you, and prayer, maybe we are getting there. I truly want the best for you because I know that you will do good things, difficult things, powerful things. I have every confidence in you. What a blessing you are.

"Parks"

Live like you love it, laugh like you got it, stand like you mean it, sing like you own it. Pray from your soul, hang on and let go, live well, my little one…"

Made in the USA
Las Vegas, NV
20 July 2022

51892672R00059